DYNAMIC SILENCE

AN INTRODUCTION TO CONCENTRATIVE MEDITATION

DYNAMIC SILENCE

AN INTRODUCTION TO CONCENTRATIVE MEDITATION

ARTHUR S. HOUGH, Ph.D.

CompCare® Publishers
2415 Annapolis Lane, Minneapolis, MN 55441

Hough, Arthur S., 1928-

Dynamic Silence: an introduction to concentrative
meditation/Arthur S. Hough.

p. cm.

"Old and new ways to reduce stress and become more
productive and creative in life."

ISBN 0-89638-235-4

1. Meditation. 2. Contemplation. 3. Stress management.
I. Title.

BF637.M4H68 1991   90-21932
155.9'042—dc20   CIP

Cover and interior design by Lois Stanfield

Inquiries, orders, and catalog requests should be addressed to:
CompCare Publishers
2415 Annapolis Lane
Minneapolis, Minnesota 55441
Call toll free 800/328-3330
(Minnesota residents 612/559-4800)

6   5   4   3   2   1
96   95   94   93   92   91

CONTENTS

Preface

I have read too many books on meditation. Thirty years ago, I went into a philosophical bookstore in San Francisco and asked the clerk for a book on meditation. He laughed and waved his hand at one entire wall of the store. "There they are," he said. "Hundreds of them." Trying to cover my embarrassment, I then asked him for the best beginner's book. I took what he handed me and fled, but I can tell you that I am still looking for the best *beginner's* book in meditation. I can't keep waiting, so I have tried to write it myself.

When I began studying meditation, I found that most meditation books told me far more about it than I really wanted to know. Most treatments connected meditation to one of the mystical disciplines. Then, in the decades of the seventies and eighties, meditation became westernized and many meditation books focused on statistical studies and psychological implications. But few practical manuals were available.

This book is a manual of immediate immersion in concentrative meditation, with great variety, a clear sequential program, and enough background information to explain what meditation is, and why it is an effective method of improving one's life. That's all.

But it is my students who finally taught me meditation. The enormous variety of their reactions to the discipline taught me what they most want to know about meditation, what works and what doesn't work.

Perhaps like you, they first approach meditation with curious skepticism. They struggle with the concepts and the exercises. Then something wonderful usually happens. They begin to ride the wave, and it carries them to a high point of excitement about meditation. But one must wait for it. Here's what a typically cautious student wrote in his log about his first ten days of meditation:

Day 1: *I've never put much stock in meditation. I feel uptight.*

Day 2: *Again, not relaxed—felt kind of silly; body tense and racing.*

Day 3: *A little more successful; I let myself relax.*

Day 4: *I feel weird about this:* awkward. *I'm trying to flow with it, but haven't been feeling very successful.*

Day 5: *I'm exhausted today, so I meditated, and OK, I feel a little better about it; my mind was clear and my body kind of relaxed.*

Day 6: *I was able to just flow with the meditating today. I'm putting away my negative feelings now, and I think I'm making progress. Today I was fairly relaxed; didn't feel tense or silly and felt clear.*

Day 7: *OK, I haven't totally fallen for meditating, but I was kind of eager to do it again today, and I was able to get all the junk out of my head, and my body didn't feel tense.*

Day 8: *Today I felt at ease during meditation. My mind was clear and I was able to relax, free from intervention.*

Day 9: *I'm easing along with meditation. Today I felt much more comfortable—not worrying about what I was supposed to get out of it. I felt completely peaceful.*

Day 10: *I think I'm regressing; I didn't feel as good as yesterday.*

I include concentrative meditation in my teaching of interpersonal and intrapersonal communication because the beneficial effects seem to come earlier and with greater intensity than they do in the more rational approaches to seeing the world more clearly. In fact, the rewards are often startling, as meditation bypasses rationality to peaceful clarity.

It is truly a dynamic silence.

ACKNOWLEDGMENTS

Although this is the first commercial edition of *Dynamic Silence*, I have published two previous versions for my students in Integrative Communication at San Francisco State University. I am indebted to their excellent feedback, and to my friend and roving amanuensis, Betty Gardiner, who edited and published these earlier editions.

I.

AN INTRODUCTION TO MEDITATION

IMMEDIATE IMMERSION

I'm assuming that you are reading this book because you would like to make some positive changes in the ways you think and feel. Perhaps you seek release of some sort from your usual tensions and mental clutter. Some people report immediate first-time effects from concentrative meditation, but no words fully describe the actual experience of meditation. You really have to feel it to know it—and there's no good reason to delay the experience while you read about it.

Before we get into the history of meditation and the benefits it offers, I'd like you to try a simple meditation *now* and feel what happens. It is easy to start meditating because you're already carrying all you need to accomplish it—your portable mind. The only other things you need are the will to meditate and the patience to wait for its rewards. If you *have* meditated before, try it again now as if it were your first experience.

Your First Meditation:
THE BREATH COUNTING MEDITATION

1. Find a reasonably quiet, pleasant, private place to sit
    and 15 uninterrupted minutes to sit there. Free your
    mind of sounds and distractions, but allow the normal
    noises of life; they need not intrude.

2. Sit comfortably straight in an upright chair, feet on the
    floor, hands resting on thighs. The key is to keep your
    spine straight.

3   Place a watch or clock where you can look at it when
    you need to.

4. Slow down your thinking, withdraw your mind to this
    place and take six long, slow breaths.

5. Begin your meditation: Close your eyes and breathe
    normally, through your nose. Your breathing will slow
    down as the meditation progresses. Silently, but with
    your fullest attention, count four breaths, like this:

    As you inhale: "AND"
    exhale: "ONE"
    inhale: "AND"
    exhale: "TWO"

    Continue counting every four breaths this way. In
    your mind, keep a running count of each group of
    four breaths. If you lose track, go back to the last num-
    ber you remember.

6. When other thoughts come along, return your atten-
    tion to your breathing and counting. Recognize distrac-
    tions and send them away courteously, without guilt or
    irritation. (The attempt to control distraction becomes

another distraction.) Scratch, yawn, shift when you need to.

7.   Stay very awake, but relaxed. Hold your posture. Work, but enjoy it.

8.   When you think of time, allow yourself to glance at your watch or clock.

9.   Stop meditating. Return to your normal thoughts and activity slowly, not abruptly. Wait a few moments before you get up and go away.

10.   Resume your normal thinking and feeling now. What happened? How did you feel before your meditation? What's different now?

Meditate again tomorrow—same time, same duration, same place, if possible. *The first time is merely a novelty; the first week, an experience; the first two weeks, a good test of the meditation.*

FIRST REWARDS

You have now learned most of the procedures of concentrative meditation: preparation, attitude, content, and follow-through. The content of the meditation is the main variable that changes as you progress from one form of meditation to another.

Keeping full attention on what you are doing by excluding distractions is the main requirement of this and all other concentrative meditations. This is the discipline you will be seeking to acquire.

But how very simple! You could have done any of the other ten meditations I'm going to suggest about as easily, but the basic purpose would have remained constant: to clear your mind through gentle concentration by focusing on the unity of some real or abstract "object."

If you worked too hard at this meditation (or not hard enough), you might feel frustrated. If you hit the stride of it, you might feel better on the first try: more relaxed, awake, energized, and broadly aware; less anxious, urgent, and annoyed.

But the problem most people have with meditation is that they expect too much too soon. If you meditate once or twice each day for two weeks, the initial good effects should become broader and deeper, physically, psychologically and, for some, spiritually.

(A student meditator on Day 1): I started my meditation today. I only meditated for a short while, I think it was about 5 minutes, and the difference I felt after completing it was amazing. Before meditating, I was in a somewhat irritated mood, then I started my meditation, breathing away slowly and easily. When I opened my eyes, I felt like another person. I was in a better mood, and I was completely relaxed. This was better than exercising.*

THE TEN-WEEK PROGRAM

In this book, we'll explore a ten-week program in concentrative meditation. Your age, sex, education, and cultural background make no significant difference to its effectiveness.

The book itself takes about an hour to read. The actual meditation time suggested is about 18 hours (if you meditate

---

*My meditation students report their reactions in written logs. From time to time throughout this book, I'll be sharing these reactions with you. All of these student entries were made during the first ten weeks of meditation.

once a day for ten weeks). Of course, if you get curious and experiment, you'll probably spend more time meditating.

Meditation is enjoyable. In fact, many people look forward to it as a daily holiday. But it's no good if you don't use it. Meditation is also a challenge and the biggest job will be sitting down to do it every day. If you miss a day, you'll tend to drop back; the continuity is lost. Meditation is not a pastime, it is a discipline with rich effects and rewards.

> *Today I realized that meditation has become an everyday necessity; it does such a wonderful thing for my state of mind; I look forward to those 15 minutes as precious time belonging only to me . . . After two days of not meditating, it was difficult to regain the calm and relaxed feeling.*

In this program of meditation you'll follow six of the most generally taught meditations (in the order of their complexity). I'll suggest a few "side trips" or meditations for occasional use. I'll also present brief passages on the background, purposes, effects, types, and uses of meditation to complement the exercises.

The Main Meditations

Weeks One and Two: Breath Counting Meditation

Weeks Three and Four: Stream Meditation

Weeks Five and Six: Single Point Meditation

Weeks Seven and Eight: 1,000 Petal Lotus Meditation

Week Nine: Mantra Meditation

Week Ten: The Zen of Doing

The Side Trips

1. Safe Harbor Meditation

2. Noise-Noise-Noise Meditation

3. Mini-Meditations

4. Sensory Meditations

5. Tai Chi Chuan (a high-power, continuous discipline)

THE BENEFITS OF MEDITATION

- To meditate is to see the world, yourself, and others in a new way.

- Meditation allows dramatic positive effects, physically, psychologically, socially, creatively and in your chosen work.

- Meditation is as positively powerful as any drug you could take, prescribed or nonprescribed.

- Meditation can open you to wider spiritual horizons.

- Meditation is safe and simple.

- Meditation works.

HOW SOON DOES MEDITATION WORK?

Most meditation programs advise two weeks to a month of practice before expecting results. I cannot promise otherwise, except to say that a significant number of my own students report measurable results in as few as six days. Be patient and don't place deadlines on the expected effects of your meditation. You might note the following comments from "new meditators":

Day 1: *I felt strange—in another world, as I opened my eyes.*

Day 2: *I felt dizzy; strange; wanted to stop.*

Day 3: *Today my body relaxed.*

Day 4: *Felt guilty—meditation isn't working.*

Day 5: *No guilt today; I felt out of this world as if I was in a world empty of thoughts; so empty I started hearing echoes of my own counting; I felt relaxed; anxiety and stress diminished. I feel more comfortable about meditation.*

Day 6: *I felt lightheaded and dozed off.*

Day 7: *I felt relaxed and cleared of stressful thoughts; all I could think of was how great I felt...in a better mood all day, calm without anxiety.*

Day 3: *In three days, strange as it sounds, I am beginning to feel better. I'm sleeping better; dreams are less violent and more pleasant.*

Day 5: *I really started to get into meditating; my reading seems to flow much easier than before; food tasted better than before; I really didn't think it would work this well. I'm looking forward to the next meditation.*

Day 12: *The first time I tried to meditate I felt confident physically. This manifested itself in my walk. I now notice a change in my decision-making process. For example, I seem to accept those who work around me just for who and what they are. And I feel that "it's okay." Also I'm trying to diet, and I notice that when I get hungry, I take the time to take a mini-meditation, and the anxious, hungry feeling dissipates. Somehow meditation helps me to understand what it is I really feel. And most of the time it's not really food, it's rest, comfort, or exercise [I need].*

Side Trip #1
SAFE HARBOR MEDITATION

Safe Harbor is one of the easiest meditations because you create it yourself and it allows your mind to move to where you'd like it to go. (I follow the Lawrence LeShan method presented in his book, *How To Meditate,* pp. 76-78.)

1.   Sit comfortably straight in any reasonably quiet place.

2.   Relax and close your eyes.

3.   Start the meditation. Imagine that there exists within you, or outside of you, a safe harbor that is yours. When you go to your harbor, you feel safe, secure, at peace, right and whole, and "at home"— needing nothing more. Now imagine that this harbor sends out a signal or a feeling that you can sense, turn toward, and drift to. Let your mind move to it, enter it, and be there—with no other action necessary on your part. Just be there, totally in this "place."

4.   Stay in your safe harbor for five or ten minutes, then return slowly to your regular thoughts and activities.

5.   What happened? How do you feel?

For the first few meditations, you may go to different places for safe harbor. Before long, you'll find the place where you feel most at home. Then, whenever you do this meditation, you can move directly to your safe harbor. Eventually, your harbor can become a safe place you look forward to visiting in meditation.

The place that opened itself to me is a partly shady clearing directly next to a brook. Also in the scene is a bridge. It's an old Japanese style, carved of plain dark wood. I wonder what it leads to, though it's not particularly imposing. It's just there for now.

My special place is on a one-man raft in a lake. I was so involved that I actually felt a soft breeze when it began to get hot.

I saw myself steering a big ship into a harbor and docking it safely. Once there, I relaxed by walking around the ship. It was immense. I was all alone. It was also foggy. A lighthouse guided me into this place.

I go to a comfortable chair I curled up in as a child.

II.

THE NATURE OF MEDITATION

MEDITATION EAST AND WEST

Both Eastern and Western meditation originated from attempts to contact God, but they follow two largely different forms. Western meditation is active and goal-directed—a way to communicate with God and ask for change. In this approach, meditation, contemplation, and prayer are closely intermingled. Eastern meditation, on the other hand, is passive. It invites us to empty our minds and quiet our egos in order to hear what God might impart to us. As such, Eastern meditation tends to be more physically and psychologically sensitizing and rewarding.

There are many kinds of Eastern spiritual meditation: some focus on internal listening, others focus on external stimuli. Meditation is a principal discipline in the many sects of the Hindu and Buddhist religions, and the Sufis. Meditation is also dominant in Western Christian monastic life. A meditating Zen Buddhist master is so into the here and now, that if a gun were to fire behind him, an electroencephalograph reading of his brain wave would show only a single blip and no follow-up! A Hindu meditator's trance would be so deep that a gunshot nearby would elicit no reaction at all!

These examples of meditative discipline illustrate the power meditation can generate even though its form may vary. Meditation need not be connected to a particular belief system to be enormously rewarding.

Until the Western world discovered the deep physical, psychological, and social gains of meditation, most books about meditation were Eastern and spiritually oriented. Today, meditation is widespread in Western countries, and it is now recognized in two forms: the spiritual (historic and religious) and the practical (enrichment without fundamental change).

Concentration and Meditation

Eastern mystics draw a distinction between "concentration" and "meditation"; they view our practical meditation, or structured exercises, as "concentration." In these terms, practical meditation is a basic training, or preparation of the mind, for real meditation. In the Chinese tradition, one practices concentration for a few years before true meditation is begun. In the West, where we rarely take time to meditate intensively with spiritual teachers, the term "meditation" has quite a different meaning. It refers primarily to the concentrative disciplines.

Why Meditation Took Root Slowly in Western Culture

When meditation was first introduced on a large scale to Western culture in the fifties, science, media, and education approached it with condescension and skepticism. Considered more radical than Western self-help therapies, meditation was often ignored—or not fully believed.

Meditation, a passive process, had to be gradually introduced into our "doing"-oriented society. In Western culture, emphasis has been placed more often on performance and outcome than on inner awareness in the moment.

A second hurdle was to integrate meditation's mystical associations into Western culture, which is governed by science and reason. Mystics who sleep on nails, stop their heartbeats, and walk on hot coals have been subject to humorous rather than serious portrayals. In order to appeal to our practical nature in Western culture, meditation has had to become less mysterious and magical, and more realistic and functional.

To complicate the matter further, meditation had earned the reputation of being a practice of counterculture groups, such as cults, sects, and gurus, whose social motives are vague and sometimes perceived as threatening to society-at-large.

Meditation was also suspect because of the emphasis our culture places on verbal communication. Unlike other forms of therapy, meditation honors silence and an inner calm not intended for—or fully describable in—words. Meditation downplays rational thinking and language.

Naturally, it has taken time for meditation to root itself in our culture. Over time, however, it passed its critical period of initiation and now is commonly accepted, applied, and/or taught in many of our social institutions. Its physical and psychological benefits are now well documented by the media, the sciences, and educators. Following are some of the more common descriptions of practical meditation:

" . . . a classic way of developing the receptive attitude. It is practice in the skill of being quiet and paying attention." (Edward Maupin, *"On Meditation"*)

" . . . a method of allowing the mind to be drawn automatically to the deepest and most refined level of thinking." (*Wall Street Journal*)

"Meditation creates an inner 'isolation chamber' . . . sheers off distracting impressions and thoughts . . .

the outer world is removed causing a 'centering.'" (Patricia Carrington, *Freedom in Meditation*)

"Meditation is called 'coming home,' a remembering . . . meditation is achieved at the point where the mind and the spirit converge." (Lawrence LeShan, *How To Meditate*)

Just in case you harbor some old biases about concentrative meditation, let's briefly review what it *is not:*

- It is not a trance-like departure from the world. We do not commonly lose touch with the here and now in concentrative meditation.

- It is not a spiritual and mystical phenomenon: *it is a psychophysical discipline.* The spiritual label is a *use* that can be applied to meditation, not a definition of it. Spirituality is one of many facets of our lives that can be enriched by meditation.

- It does not "weaken" the will or restructure the personality. It serves to expand our present consciousness.

- It is not an interruption of nor a splitting off from the flow of life, but a process that adds perspective to one's present life.

- It is not addictive, antisocial or antidemocratic. It is a step toward unity, at all levels, not divisiveness.

THE MIND'S ROLE IN MEDITATION

It's becoming more evident that the useful, pleasant, durable, and even dramatic effects of meditation have a single cause: a clearer, more alert mind. Using nothing more than a deliberate minimal shift in consciousness, you can experience these results:

- immediate reduction in stress

- sharper perception

- an unusual sense of awakening

- a dimming out of time

- a release from compulsiveness and repression

- increased tranquility and tolerance for self and others

- an increase in self-regard

- an improvement in problem-solving skills

- a distinct feeling of creativity

Add these positive results to other known effects of meditation, and we can trust that we're looking at some single, but major, shift in mind—either the addition of something new or the recovery of something forgotten. Three prominent theories of meditation appear to explain this phenomenon:

- that perhaps meditation shifts responsibility from one part of the mind to another. One hypothesis suggests that it shifts or re-focuses mental functions from the left hemisphere of the brain to the right hemisphere.

- that meditation might involve a reduction in the ego, the sense of one's separate self. This "turning down" of our habitual personal control makes room for new responses.

- that meditation creates a temporary transcendence or temporary suspension of one's world view. The result is a new perspective—a new ability to see beyond our normal, limited world view.

Hemisphere Interplay

Recent brain research suggests that we have two functional brains, one in the left hemisphere and one in the right. The left hemisphere mostly directs the verbal, problem-solving, and daily activities of our minds. This left hemisphere tends to respond better to direct command than does the right hemisphere. The right hemisphere specializes in abstract and spatial concepts, both of which are closest to actual perception.

These findings propose that a shift between the left and right brain hemispheres offers new ways to comprehend reality. Such a shift creates a portable second mind that doesn't speak to us as loudly as the first. This "mind" is like a symphony orchestra playing in a nearby park next to a noisy hurdy-gurdy in the street. The orchestra music, though always present, can't be heard until the hurdy-gurdy subsides. This second mind is also like the stars: always in the sky, but not seen until the daylight dims. It's as though we must "dim" the external light of our busy minds to see the stars within us.

This harmonizing of the two hemispheres, or "shift" from the left to the right hemisphere, can be accessed through meditation. In fact, when the alpha brain wave (commonly associated with meditation) is monitored during meditation, it sweeps forward rapidly from the back to the front of the left hemisphere, and then repeats this in the right hemisphere. The alpha wave's sweeping motion is thought to produce the integrative harmony we experience in meditation.

Meditation as Surrender

It is possible to be too "self" conscious to meditate, for we do not *win* at meditation or succeed in it as we do in other mental and physical tests. Meditation is not an application of the ego, but an *abdication* of it. In meditation, we are asked to "let go," a nontask requiring passivity of ego and paradigm. If all the meditator can think of is "Here I am, meditating . . . How am I doing? . . . I really did well today!" he or she has not let go of ego, the mundane mind. And this is the paradox of meditation: it requires us to be fully aware, without effort or self-congratulation, momentarily dropping emphasis on who we are. Feelings of personal success will corrupt the process of meditation—like walking on your own garden after you have planted it.

For our purposes, we'll refer to dropping one's grip on self-image and ego as "ego de-automatization." We start with the premise that the ego seems to control our conscious thoughts. This ego is but a *portion* of the real self. Once we free ourselves from the ego's grip, we gain access to deeper parts of our real selves. We are, however, highly protective of our own self-image and our world view, and the ego often insists that we not release these self-images.

"When too large a portion of our experience is automatized," psychologist Arthur Deikman has said, "we become walking bundles of habits."[1]

In meditation training, the ego is repeatedly depicted as a principal distraction or barrier. In her book, *Freedom in Meditation,* Patricia Carrington notes that, "Up to a certain point the ego seems to serve us—beyond that we may start to serve *it.* If the ego is in the driver's seat *all* the time, then direct experience fades away."[2]

So we learn that we must surrender and quiet the ego and approach reality without its resistance.

The story is told of a European professor who called on a Zen master to seek truth, yet who spent his visit telling how much he knew. When the master served tea, he kept pouring, even though the visitor's cup overflowed. The professor finally complained, "My cup's overfull! No more will go in!" to which the master replied: "Like this cup, you are full of your own opinions and speculations. How can I show you Zen unless you first empty your cup?"

De-automatization, or "letting go," does not result in a loss or regression. Instead, de-automatization creates a permission that we give ourselves to drop our stereotyped organization of self and reality. By "letting go," we can use our mental faculties in new and advanced ways.

"A NEW PERSPECTIVE"

When the emphasis in meditation is on "lifting" one's perception of reality as a whole, then a paradigm shift, or transcendence, occurs.

Each of us apparently adopts, between ages seven to ten, a central world view, or paradigm. In Western culture, each of us apparently chooses one of several major paradigms. Thereafter, this paradigm arranges all of our mental categories into a single organization dictated by a master metaphor.[3]

Our paradigms give us our marvelously structured and organized view of external reality, others, and ourselves. But our paradigms are limiting, for they have the effect of screening reality. They distort, reject, and modify that which does not fit the way we *know* the world to be. We are, then, both served *and* limited by our paradigms.

There are breakthroughs we can experience that give us perspectives on our paradigms, without losing their benefits: peak experience, crisis reaction, meditation, and hypnosis are some examples. The benefits of a new perspective on our paradigm are nearly identical to the positive effects of meditation: expanded perception; reduced anxiety and dogmatism; increased tolerance, creativity, and self-worth (to name a few).

Meditation, then, may be explained as the quieting of the paradigm, its tightly held beliefs, and its firmly categorized ego image.

One thing seems clear: Meditation does not touch off a set of scattered phenomena. Rather, it adjusts some governing core of thought. This central core, under meditation, gives way to a more expansive perception, one that emphasizes unity over separation, and freedom over restraint.

Freeing ourselves from ego and world view dogmatism usually takes years of therapy or intellectual study! Meditation appears to produce the same effects by bypassing such long and rigorous processes.

> **Day 4:** *Meditation gives me a sense of humor that I struggled for previously. It helps me go to a place where I can see the relative significance of things that boast of their importance in my life and then try to tangle me up . . . My ability to laugh is doing me so much good.*

Side Trip #2
THE NOISE-NOISE-NOISE MEDITATION

Distraction is the biggest challenge in the early stages of meditation. Here is a meditation that turns distraction into the meditation itself. *Distraction will be the content of the meditation.*

1. Find a quiet place to sit comfortably straight.

2. Place a timepiece where you can glance at it.

3. Slow down, relax, and take six long, slow breaths.

4. Start the meditation:
    A. Allow yourself to breathe from the abdomen. Watch your abdomen as it rises and falls. (You ought to have at least one meditation in which you "contemplate your navel.") Attend entirely to your breathing.
    B. As you acknowledge your breathing movements, also acknowledge thoughts, sensations, and emotions that enter your consciousness. *One at a time.* As each new thought appears, capture it in a single word or two, and repeat that single word or two three times, once on each breath. *Noise, noise, noise. Hungry, hungry, hungry, Worried, worried, worried.* Give your full attention to each distracting thought as you repeat it. After each distraction, concentrate on your breathing until the next thought appears.

5. Meditate for ten minutes.

6. Stop meditating and return to your normal thoughts and actions slowly.

7. What happened? How do you feel?

REFERENCES

1. Quoted in Carrington, *Freedom in Meditation,* p. 313.

2. Ibid., p. 312.

3. Arthur Hough, *The Forgotten Choice,* 1988. Copyrighted and self-published.

III.

THE REWARDS OF MEDITATION

A person is not likely to *continue* meditating for its own sake, out of shallow curiosity, or by prescription from others. None of these motivations would sustain a beginner for long. The beginning meditator needs to examine some of the possible purposes and effects of meditation. Why would one meditate?

Perhaps more convincing than the centuries of literature on meditation are some of the comments made by 120 university students who volunteered in 1988-90 to follow the concentrative meditation program outlined in this book. Many of these comments (selected from written logs) are made in complete amazement by these new meditators, who had been meditating for less than two weeks. Let's look at the ongoing phenomena reported firsthand by these beginning meditators:

1. Peace, Serenity, Release from Tension, Relaxation:

> **Day 5:** *Initially I couldn't relax, which caused me to breathe fast, and then faster. Finally I stopped to collect my thoughts and to relax. I started off slowly and gradually*

began to relax and to concentrate. Right now I feel so good. I feel so relaxed. After the meditation I just sat in the chair and daydreamed for a few minutes. I didn't want to come back. I truly felt as though I was somewhere else and wanted to stay. My mind felt free and unclogged from problems, stress, etc. Physically I didn't want to move . . . I really felt still.

Day 6: I got into an argument with two of my friends today, so I went to my room and meditated. Something strange happened. I felt my whole energy of my body go to my head, and it felt heavy and light at the same time. It was cool. I felt real excited afterwards, like something profound had happened to me.

Day 7: I felt a great sense of peace, a sort of lifting sensation. I had found it before; I found the place that makes it happen.

Day 10: While I meditate I feel I'm on another planet—so silent. I feel so relaxed, so clear; I have a smile on my face. The more I meditate, the more I love myself. I couldn't wait to get home and meditate to forget everything that went on today—and be totally clear. Sometimes I'm sleepy afterwards; sometimes I get a burst of power. I relax so easily now.

2. Energy, Exhilaration, Feeling Refreshed:

Day 2: Great effects today! Feel ready to take on anything!

Day 3: Every muscle in my body was relaxed while every cell in my brain was alive! This is the greatest feeling. I can't believe how much of a better mood I've been in. I love it!

Day 7: I can feel bursts of negative energy running through and out of my body and positive energy flowing *back in to replace the negative's void.*

Day 8: *I meditated to procrastinate from my work; it made the day! I feel like working on everything now.*

Day 11: *Ten minutes out of one day gives me eighteen full hours of sheer energy! Wow!*

3. Timelessness:

Day 6: *Today I didn't even want to come out of it. I felt like I was in such a comfortable place and position. I just wanted to stay there. It went by too fast today. The time just flew by, but when the 15 minutes was up, I did stop. I really felt comfortable, and it helped me with the rest of the day.*

Day 10: *I felt as though I'd slipped through a hole in time. I was falling softly through benign warm clouds of pinkish mist. I stayed longer than usual, probably about 10 solid minutes actually within this state.*

4. Clarity, Organization, Concentration:

Day 4: *My concentration was the best it's ever been today. Everything seems lighter, as though a weight had been lifted from my shoulders.*

Day 7: *Before the meditation I had been studying political science for six hours. My mind was full and run down. However, after the meditation, I had a clearer mind and a more energetic mind. It seems that the meditation allowed the thoughts cluttering my mind to dissipate. Perhaps I should meditate every so often when doing homework for long periods of time.*

5. Self-Satisfaction, Self-Worth:

Day 6: *I guess this meditation teaches me not to be mad at myself.*

Day 6: *I feel mightier than I've ever been. I have a great sense of open-mindedness to many directions. It's been less than a week, but I can already feel a great sense of self-confidence.*

Day 7: *It worked! It worked! I actually came out of this stupid meditation exercise feeling good and not angry with myself. I did it right before I was going out (mainly because I was so jittery over the evening that lay ahead), and 15 minutes later, I swear, I felt really, incredibly relaxed, yet relaxed in a good way, not a sleepy relaxed way . . . I'm not as strange as I thought. I was beginning to think I was immune to just about everything.*

Day 7: *Meditation is fantastic. I want to say that my breathing rate has improved dramatically. My posture is getting much better. Both mentally and physically I feel great. It's been a week today, and at the end of each day I look forward to unwinding by meditating. No phone calls, no one at the door. My roommate knows not to come in when I'm meditating. I feel wonderful.*

Day 8: *I like this new experience of meditation because I'm different for some reason and I like the change. When I start to feel depressed, I can now control it.*

Day 12: *Okay, I'm feeling good right now because I did my meditation, and now, one hour later, I'm still feeling relaxed and feel like I haven't got a care in the world. That's incredibly rare for me, mind you, so I've got a good reason to be so thrilled.*

6. Self-Awareness:

Day 5: *I was able to feel my heartbeat and count in time. I feel very aware of myself and my movements.*

Day 7: *I am noticing my heartbeat and the tightness of my jaw (almost teeth grinding).*

Day 12: *I meditated long and hard today. I was really upset with my parents, and I was crying. I felt like there was nowhere to go or nothing that I could do. But you know what? I sat in my car, which was parked in the garage, and I meditated. I concentrated and breathed. You know what I found out? After I meditated, I found myself at fault, not my parents. My mood swing had done a full 360 degrees, and I was on top of the world! No one knew what had come over me! Or what was so unusual about me, but they don't know about meditation! They don't know what they are missing. This is wonderful.*

7. Patience, Tolerance, Acceptance of Others:

Day 5: *I am much calmer and less judgmental than before I started meditation.*

Day 9: *A successful session, following a disastrous one the day before. Lately I've been noticing myself being a bit more patient when dealing with people. My shyness also seems to be wearing away since I've been saying "Howdy" to people in my classes I barely know . . . I'm beginning to notice a difference.*

Undated log: *I seem to see the world through another perspective. I have learned so much about myself, and this in turn has helped me to see beauty in the people around me. I hate to sound corny, but I feel so peaceful. I love my children in a greater degree. I understand and I'm more* *willing to deal with my anger when it comes to my husband and the rest of the family.*

8. Body Changes, Sensitivity:

Day 11: *I felt so light and airy it was as if I were floating like a feather.*

Day 11: *I calmed a stomachache and turned from being very tired to being rested and more awake.*

Day 11: *I stopped a ringing in my ear just by relaxing and concentrating.*

Day 12: *I feel light as a cloud. All the immediate pressures of my life seem less threatening to me. Today, I also notice every detail of sound in my environment, even the quality or feel of silence around me.*

Day 14: *After meditating, just at first I felt some weird feeling going through my body. But it was good—wonderful and peaceful. Nothing bad. I just felt like I was floating along on a river, calmly and serenely. I didn't want to leave my meditation spot. I was just too comfortable.*

LASTING RETURNS OF MEDITATION

We've examined the relatively superficial benefits that a person might expect in the first weeks of meditation. Each benefit is rewarding in its own way. But there are more enduring, traditional, and deeper effects to be gained from concentrative meditation. The following benefits of meditation make it deeply rewarding:

1. Centering and Self-Worth

"Centering" describes a sense of wholeness, self-regard, and a merging of internal contradictions. Centering brings with it a sense of peace, tolerance, and spontaneity. It reduces anxiety, self-criticism, and the need to prove to yourself or others who you are. Meditators report all of these gains as well as a greater sense of control over their lives. Meditation is not psychotherapy, because it does not alter basic personality characteristics. But meditation does tend to enhance one's overall sense of well-being, and in that sense it can transform one's life.

> **Undated log:** *I feel lifted—more confident about myself; my face relaxes; I feel a certain serenity; I feel more aware of who I am, more self-assured. Meditation to me is how to listen to myself and my real needs.*

> **Day 13:** *I wasn't as emotional as last night, and I feel rather positive. I'm positive because my inner feelings are being revealed. I'm being allowed to see them, and now it's up to me to be able to deal with them. I like this . . . It seems as though the meditation allows repressed feelings to surface, because I'm the type who tends to take in a lot of "mess" . . . and then when I get upset it explodes. To me, this meditation is saying, "Hey, these are your feelings. Deal with them no matter how awful they are." It's allowing me to think and open my eyes to myself. It's allowing me to ask myself questions and to explore myself . . . I don't know if it's from the meditation, but I tell you, I'm trying to deal with "me," myself, and find out what I want.*

2. Discovery of Our True Nature

When we release our limited world views of reality and other people in meditation, we also release our habitual ways of perceiving *ourselves.* Cultural overlays of who we are recede; even our vocabularies and our sense of past and future appear to dim out. It is not so much that we are deprived of our old ways of seeing ourselves, others, and reality. Instead, our old ways of seeing seem to expand in that we begin to see beyond our habitual world views. Meditators develop new ways of perceiving and reacting to the world around them.

> **Day 12:** *I felt like reality hit me in the face. All of a sudden I felt really emotional and started centering on the here and now. It seemed like my negative feelings wanted to come out. They wanted to emerge to the surface. It was as if my inner self was telling me that I have to deal with my negative feelings, because I do have them. It was really weird.*

> **Day 12:** *During the day following my meditation I saw things in a new light. The grass looked more alive and the air smelled like candy. When I looked in the mirror, I saw my inside, not just my outside. I felt as though I really made a change in my life today.*

3. Unification

Human thought leans toward differentiating between things. We learn to see differences and then to categorize those differences. Meditation helps us focus on unity: First, we begin to see ourselves as a true unity, and then we begin to feel a sense of harmony with everything around us. This is a very personal, often cosmic sense of unity in which the meditator feels an intense belonging and harmony with all things. The final effect of this unity is often reported as a feeling of universal and uncritical love.

> **Undated log:** *So many adjectives, but the best one to describe this is "serenity." I have never felt so at peace with myself, others and, in fact, everything.*

Day 7: *It seems second nature to me today. I look forward to it . . . I feel very "whole" today.*

4. Worship

Traditionally, worship has been a primary objective of meditation, though not a necessary purpose or effect. A more thorough discussion on the spiritual effects of meditation can be found on page 39.

I can feel the air around my body and it seems very spiritual, as though my body is some type of "spiritual shield." It's an unusual yet a very comforting feeling.

5. Creativity in Thought, Action, and Art

Those who practice meditation claim to create and perform better as a result. They are known to memorize lists and solve arithmetic problems better. This ability to "think more clearly" seems to be related to a change in cognitive awareness. Meditation yields both a general improvement in academic performance and an experience of greater efficiency.

Although meditation doesn't turn non-creative people into creative ones, it does provide an inner solitude and perceptual openness that's linked to creative thought. Meditators report being more "egoless" during creative periods: When we disconnect our egos from our narrow personal desires, we spark our creative freedom.

Day 7: *Today before singing at a wedding I was a bit impatient, wanting it to start on time and wanting to rehearse a song that I wasn't familiar with. I chose to take a mini- meditation for about five minutes in the car. Need-*

*less to say, the song went beautifully well. I was able to let
go of the anxiety and pick up creativity instead.*

Undated log: *After meditating these eight weeks, I now
see an improvement in my writing skills. I guess I'm not
afraid to say what I feel is appropriate. I guess I'm not as
judgmental; the words just spill out.*

6. Stress Reduction and Health

It's known that meditation slows the heart down. During meditation, the lungs use less oxygen and the brain emits an alpha
wave. Brain waves assume an unusually even and rhythmic
form during meditation — all areas of the brain appear to har-
monize and pulsate together. Electrical skin responses lower,
indicating reduced anxiety. Tension headaches and insomnia
subside. Overall, a low-stress state is achieved.

Day 3: *Wow! Today was the best meditation I have had; it
more than made up for the bad meditation I had yesterday. I was much more in control of my thoughts. I also
noticed I was able to focus on my counting and breathing
a lot easier. Outside thoughts keep entering, but I was able
to push them aside and focus on my counting. This meditation didn't even seem that long. I just opened my eyes,
and it was already 18 minutes. I was surprised. After opening my eyes, everything seemed like it was in slow motion.
It seemed like I was just coming back into my body. I felt so
relaxed and peaceful. After I emerged from my meditation, I felt like I had more energy. Also, this meditation
somewhat rectified the stress in my life. I had a bad day at
work, and this meditation helped. I also forgot to mention
my body felt even lighter this time.*

7. Release of Untapped Potential

Meditation apparently helps us tap into a new, mysterious source of energy. It induces a sense of deep relaxation and a highly alert mental state. Physical perception is also more sharply focused: water is wetter and colors are brighter.

As self-regard and centering are enhanced, so are spontaneity, self-actualization, and a capacity for intimate contact. The discipline gained through meditation appears to strengthen will, purpose, and goal-guided behavior. Previously unrecognized potentials rise to the surface.

> ***Day 10:*** *I feel really great, wide awake and exhilarated. I perceive things like smells with great awareness. My roommate tells me I am more relaxed, and he thinks I am on drugs.*

8. Pleasure

In addition to being so enjoyable that people look forward to it daily, meditation also appears to enhance serenity, love, zest, joy, sensuality, and sexual interest.

> *I feel so relaxed right now and happy. I just drifted into the meditation and it seems so natural, like something I always do. I saw a few colors, namely purple and some white.*

> *Meditation brings me awareness of my posture, and every motion is dance, and there's a fine golden thread going straight up from the very top of my head, gently lifting me, lightening me.*

> *I feel so much better, refreshed, calmer. If someone told me a month ago I'd be meditating and enjoying it this much, I'd have laughed in their face.*

What a nice little vacation. It doesn't cost any money; there are no time hassles; I have control. Meditation is conscious self- control.

IV.

MEDITATION AND A BETTER LIFE

There are long-term personal effects of meditation that extend beyond actual meditation sessions. People who meditate tend to develop an openness to life. They become tolerant of their own shortcomings, develop a healthy perspective on their problems, and become amazingly efficient. They are less likely to engage in self-blame.

> *I attribute to the meditation that lately I have been more complacent under heavy stress, happier and more concentrated. I can stretch the fifteen minutes to seem like an hour. When I open my eyes, it's like opening them for the first time in the morning.*

Both during and after meditation, people tend to take the "charge" off current concerns and problems—and not just one problem at a time, but many problems simultaneously. Meditation can have the effect of lifting some psychological repressions because it helps bring long-buried memories to the surface.

Meditators tend to be more open to others; they are less needful to be the center of attention and are reported to be easier to live with. (Some meditators use it with guests, inviting them to group meditation before dinner; it tends to reduce role-playing.)

> **Day 9:** *For some reason I feel that meditation has not only helped me out personally, but also in my social life. My girlfriend has told me I am a more relaxed individual. She feels I am communicating more and that I am not as tense as I usually am. People at work have noticed a difference also. It's funny, because there are three people on my staff and all of them meditate, and they are helping me along as I go through these exercises, and I even feel we are working better as a team.*

There is less psychic drag in persons who meditate. They evidence a sense of forward movement or flow, intense concentration, and the quality of being lost in the game of life: fully absorbed in what they are doing and in control of their actions. They report that time seems to dissolve and distractions disappear. On a larger scale, meditation may reduce one's use of foods or participation in environments or activities that run counter to the individual's natural rhythms. Meditation seems to shift a person's emphasis away from compulsive accomplishing and toward simply "living."

> *At the place I work I usually race around, thinking too fast, stopping in the middle of doing something and thinking what else I need. But lately I've slowed my pace down and have not had such lapses in memory recently. It used to be frustrating and it happens still, but not as frequently since I began meditation. Hopefully I will be able to get rid of the memory lapse and continually slow my pace if I continue to meditate.*

Meditation is also known to help people to accept death peacefully through the lessening of pain, depression, and anxiety; it helps reduce the fear of dying.

MEDITATION AND WORK

Improved physical and psychological health will obviously enhance our work lives. Many people who meditate find that it "opens the floodgates" of their minds and produces more creative thoughts.

Meditation seems to extend our endurance level so that we can sustain long periods of creative work. Meditation "recharges our batteries" and actually helps us become more fully committed to projects, events, and relationships. It helps us emphasize internal, over external, rewards. Meditation helps us feel more united with our environment, and with our past, present, and future.

> **Day 6:** *After meditating, I started to study my textbook by re-reading the chapters I had highlighted. The meditation seemed to increase the duration of my attention span, because I studied for four hours straight.*

> **Undated log:** *After meditating this morning I went to work. I always expect myself to have a bad day at work . . . But I told myself that I wasn't going to let anyone bother me . . . (a customer, fellow employee or supervisor). I tried not to let them affect me. Whenever somebody said something, . . . I would listen to it, respond and then let it go. I always returned to the peaceful state of mind. It seemed like I worked the whole day with a smile on my face. One assistant manager commented on how [much] fuller my face was. I ended up coming home in a very good mood, which is quite unusual [for me] especially after work.*

Many large U.S. corporations recognize the benefits of meditation and have established meditation rooms in the workplace. Many employees now use meditation at work breaks and before brainstorming sessions.

Meditation and Deep Listening

For those in helping professions, meditation offers distinct advantages. It seems to sharpen the ability to sense the moods and needs of others. Meditation also improves the ability to generate new and accurate insights into other people's problems. Meditators seem able to be attentive to others for longer periods of time and they are better able to cope with the negative emotions of others, including hostility. Meditation encourages an openness that sustains empathy, the ability to feel *with* another person as though his or her feelings were your own.

> *(Effects on waitressing in a restaurant): I certainly have not mastered a "mellow attitude," but I feel I do at times fall into a not-so-hectic state of mind. And I love it when I'm in that state of mind. I enjoy the customers more, and work is simply more enjoyable. I think to myself, "Why are you moving so quickly? Take it one step at a time." Then I'll take charge and slow my pace down both physically and mentally. What I really want is to be able to be in that state of mind at all times.*

Meditation as a Processing Period

Most of us would admit that we're often too busy to take time out for our own welfare. We enjoy little privacy, solitude, or reflective time in which to process the many problems and bits of information present in our daily lives.

> *I woke up as from a semi-dream, feeling that it's so nice to take time for myself, to be alone and at rest with my mind.*

Meditation appears to provide an island for busy people, a personal isolation chamber where they can process themselves, their relationships, their work, and their perceptions of reality. We need these "time-outs" to process our lives. The constant high stimulus of a normal busy life needs to be offset by periods of low stimulus for catch-up, or digestion of data and the processing of feelings.

> **Day 7:** *This had to have been the worst day of my life [at work]! I was so stressed when I came home I thought I was going to lose it and go off the deep end. When I came home from work, the first thing I did was meditate! And believe me, every bubble that I let come to mind was: stress, hate, pissed-off, upset, bad energy. When I was finished after half an hour, someone could have dropped a bomb near me, and I would not even have flinched. All the bad energy was gone.*

The Wall Street Journal quotes a thirty-one-year-old partner in a Wall Street brokerage firm, testifying to his eighteen-month experience with meditation:

> "I find myself in harmony with my surroundings. Anxiety does not affect me, and I'm less critical of people than before. You look around and think everyone else has changed, until you realize you're the one who's done the changing."

As humans, we're the only species to observe a regular seventeen-hour period of continuous wakefulness. Animals catnap, but we human beings force ourselves to stay awake. Measurements of human consciousness reveal that we tend to drop into reverie at roughly one-and-a-half-hour intervals throughout the day. Many of us use these periods of "reverie" for coffee breaks, eating, smoking, or daydreaming. Meditators are likely to use these periods of time for mini-meditations.

It should not surprise us to read that a recent Harvard University study has found that elderly people (with an average

age of 91) who were taught Transcendental Meditation, lived longer than the parallel groups who were taught other relaxation techniques, or none at all.

So, why meditate? Why meditate, indeed! Meditation appears to offer some surprisingly rich gift of life that is no farther from any of us than a quiet room and the decision to use it.

MEDITATION AND THE BODY

There is not yet enough data to report accurately what effects meditation has on sports participation (and viceversa,) but it seems likely that athletic activity may stimulate a form of meditation. Michael Murphy, who has studied the similarity between athletics and meditation, has revealed linkages between meditation and the sports of football, baseball, golf, sky and ocean diving, race car driving, mountain climbing, and distance running. Here are the linkages Murphy suggests between meditation and these sports:

- "extraordinary clarity, sometimes accompanied by a sense of slow motion;

- unusual focus and concentration;

- a sense of emptiness or nothingness;

- a release from habitual ways of seeing, or de-automatization;

- a perception of oneness and equality with everything;

- an access to larger insights, energies, and behaviors; and

- ecstasy, delight, and supreme aesthetic enjoyment."

All of these phenomena are reported as symptoms of deep meditation as well.

MEDITATION AND SPIRITUALITY

Concentrative meditation is not the most advanced form of meditation. It does, however, reach deep into the individual and causes powerful changes in perception.

Transcendence is one perceptual change that is sought after and possible to attain through meditation. Transcendence can be explained in two ways, yet ultimately it cannot be explained at all. Transcendence defies description because it incorporates an elevated state of mind and being that appears to elude us, in this sense: "That which is above can comprehend that which is below, but that which is below cannot comprehend that which is above."

Intellectually, the meditator transcends his or her normal paradigm, and in so doing perceives newness in the world, in others, and in himself or herself. Biased views are replaced by an awareness of unity and harmony. This natural balance of joy and serenity stimulates the most optimistic and positive of human hopes. It seeks a natural perfection and is accompanied by emotional peaks of ecstasy and serenity.

Spiritually, in most advanced meditations, the meditator also seeks a unity of spirit and contact with God (however God is defined by that meditator).

In both intellectual and spiritual terms, there is the quiet assurance that transcendence releases an individual's highest potential. This leads to reports of mystical, or exceptional, powers of concentration, physical capacities, and universal communication. Because the spiritual implications of transcendence are so powerful—and sometimes confusing—most spiritual leaders urge meditators to seek guidance from a teacher, guru, or master.

Naturally, meditation can be misused. It might sometimes be employed as a means of creating docile, easily manipulated individuals in the service of a leader or group more interested in imposing control than in encouraging personal freedom. Newer cults, sects, and religions appear to be more vulnerable to these manipulations than are traditional religions. For whatever purpose and in whichever context, the ideal search is one for unity with others; personal power is a secondary reward.

Once you try the ten-week program and find that it serves you well, you may wish to explore the spiritual rewards of meditation. The exercises in this book will help you get started on the practical level of life enhancement.

Side Trip #3
MINI-MEDITATIONS

A mini-meditation can add a few moments of refreshing therapy to your day. You may use any meditational form you like for a mini-meditation. My favorite is single point meditation because of its wide choice in subject matter and its emphasis on the here and now.

Standing, sitting, lying down, or walking, focus on an object with full alertness and relaxation, but without verbal thought. The object may be at hand or far away, such as a waving flag, a telephone pole, a salt-shaker, a pattern on the ceiling. Just be sure that the object is stable and directly in your line of sight.

The meditation may last as little as a minute and seldom longer than five; the occasions for it are endless:

when you first enter the house

between television shows

during breaks in conferences, workshops, or classes

after every chapter you read in a book

before writing a letter or making a phone call

before tests, examinations, performances, or competitions

The most appropriate occasion I have found for a mini-meditation is while I'm *waiting,* for waiting automatically slows me down. Also, the frustration of waiting comes from resisting rather than joining the delay. Consider meditating while waiting in lines, while waiting for service at a restaurant, while waiting for transportation or for someone who's late, or while waiting for water to boil.

A "coffee-break" meditation is a reviving experience. When you are working hard and using a lot of energy, or when your work is frustrating or annoying, make a deliberate attempt to find a quiet place for a five-minute meditation. There are empty rooms.

But privacy is not absolutely necessary for a mini-meditation. You can meditate among people so as not to draw attention to yourself. Simply be still, no matter what your posture. To avoid the distraction of thinking that people are watching you when you meditate, carry some reading material, and act as if you are reading.

The mini-meditation stops us when we are caught up in our own busy-ness. It allows us to digest incoming data without having to react instantly and, as such, improves both decisions and disposition.

Something upset me very much today; I sat down, closed my eyes and found myself meditating. Within minutes I was relaxed and felt much better.

Today I meditated in the car; the traffic was not moving, it was at a standstill so I started meditating. I was in a terrible mood, the rain and traffic was causing my temper to fume. After I started the breathing and meditating, I felt wonderful. The traffic didn't bother me so much, and the rain looked great. I love meditating!

REFERENCES

Michael Murphy, "News from Esalen: Sport as Yoga," *Esalen Institute Catalogue* Fall, 1977. p.74

Jacob Needleman, *The New Religions.* New York: Crossroads Publishing Co., 1984.

Ken Wilber, *Eye to Eye, The Quest for the New Paradigm.* New York: Anchor Press/Doubleday, 1983.

V.

HOW TO MEDITATE

There is no single way to meditate. From trances to Sufi whirls, each style of meditation offers a door into the same inner world and has something positive to offer. However, concentrative meditation is the common denominator of most advanced meditations. In order to practice concentrative meditation well, you will need to consider these six factors:

1. Setting

2. Attitude

3. Expectations and Distractions

4. Timing

5. Posture and Breathing

6. The Content-less Thought

SETTING

Whether you're indoors or out, you'll need a reasonably quiet and tranquil setting. The usual sounds of a house, apartment, or outdoor urban setting will not prohibit meditation. These sounds will simply be absorbed or dissolved, like all other distractions.

If indoors, silence the telephone and ask others not to disturb you for a half-hour. Tell those you live with that you meditate. Don't keep it a dark secret that makes you nervous when others are nearby. You will, however, need privacy at first. Meditate in solitude.

The ideal meditation nook is a pleasant, quiet place in your home with minimal sound and visual distractions. Go to your nook only when you meditate. Eventually, this spot will become a sanctuary that puts you in a meditative mood whenever you enter it.

HERE COMES THE CAT! Cats love meditation, and they're enormously drawn to people who are meditating. Those who own cats usually find them in their laps after meditation. One meditator has to put the cat outdoors during sessions—otherwise, it will claw insistently at the door of her room when she is meditating.

ATTITUDE

You can wash the dishes without wanting to, but you cannot meditate without your own full consent. Some people simply refuse to meditate, or they learn it and quit. In fact, a person can follow the instructions of meditation perfectly, but if the fragile meditative mood is not present, they will not have been meditating.

Referring to the greatest rewards of meditation, one mystic has said, "It is closest to those who desire it intensely."

The key to the meditative mood is *alert passivity,* a difficult attitude to achieve deliberately. In meditation, the object is not to win, but to "join with." It takes an agreeable surrendering of the ego. Some people fight this in attitude, posture, and in the way they follow meditation directions.

The meditative attitude lies less in what we are achieving than in what we are letting go. We do not know what we'll achieve until we get it—we only know what we'll need to give up. During the meditation itself, we need to:

- stop requiring

- stop knowing

- stop planning

- stop remembering

- stop "doing" the world

EXPECTATIONS AND DISTRACTIONS

We usually measure ourselves by whether or not we're succeeding or failing. These expectations surface whenever we start a new venture. In meditation, we need to let these expectations go. They'll only block our efforts. When we let go of the success/failure distraction, we can expect to:

Give up our world view and ego dominance

Since we rely on our world view and ego to organize our thoughts, giving them up takes time and patience. Ideally, the meditator is non-striving and non-pushing in this quest—he or she transcends, rather than stamps out, thoughts. It's common to strive for correctness; yet, to do so is self-defeating.

One mystic said, "If any man cannot grasp this matter, let him be idle and the matter will grasp him."[1]

Think of meditation as you would prayer—a continuous discipline that leads to gradual long-term change. In a long walk to its oasis, focus on the oasis. Let your feet stumble as they will.

Undated log: *I'm thinking words too much; I think I'm trying too hard—but I get tons of energy afterward.*

Expect to have good and poor sessions

Meditation teachers warn against expecting early success. Yet, my own students often report feelings of accomplishment as early as the very first day or week of meditation. This is satisfying, but sets up the false expectation of gradual, daily improvement. This is seldom the case. One day may be excellent, the next a disaster, and the third, entirely different. (Meditators who are extremely worried, feeling unwell, or very tired find it most difficult to meditate in the early days.)

Although meditation is generally pleasant, there will be dry and dull periods. These periods of resistance will lead to deeper, richer levels of concentration. One master has said, "Some people will do anything for their own advancement except work for it." Do not be among those. Endure with gentle persistence.

Expect both annoyance and unwanted entertainment

Getting rid of the small annoyances of house and street sounds, physical itches, and sudden awareness of your obligations of life are quickly dealt with in meditation. The *real* distractions are much more cunning and tenacious than these. After these early annoyances, we fall into problem-solving, then into self-entertaining fantasies, then we complain that we are bored (for boredom is the rebellion of a mind that expects something and doesn't get it). The more we expect from meditation, the more bored we can become. And when the ego realizes that its expectations are not being fulfilled, it "produces" fulfillment itself, with fantasy.

> *I'm back to counting and breathing. I really got into it today. I let go of my expectations with every exhale. Every time something came up I just blew it out. I didn't make myself wrong for things coming up. I just let them out . . . After the time was up, I felt good, and for the first time really felt I accomplished something in the meditation.*

To listen to our larger mind, we have to gently quiet the anxious, active mind, which our world view and ego control The active mind struggles to retain its voice. The active mind struggles not to be quieted, and many distractions are created by the mind struggling to evade the meditation.

To distract you, the mind may turn simple meditation instruction into a mental circus. Or, it might turn to physical discomfort, external interruptions, worries, guilt, or future plans. Its most cunning trick is to seem to comply with the meditative attitude, yet to engage in physical or psychological clowning. This clowning happens as our minds distract us with distorted images or seductive rewards:

> vivid lights and colors
> daydreams
> sudden smells
> tingling
> vibrations

"goose-bumps"
floating and out-of-body sensations
extrasensory perception
temperature changes
psychic "highs"

Such "sirens" of meditation have been well known for centuries. They are called *Makyos* or *Siddhas*. It is generally agreed that to seek such sensations, or to feel successful when they appear, only slows down inner achievement.

One *Makyo* story appears so frequently and variously in meditative literature that it has reached the level of folklore: *The student comes to his master in great excitement to report that in his recent meditations, the Virgin Mary (or Buddha, or a great White Light) appeared and sat with him in his meditative cell. The master answers, without enthusiasm, "If you concentrate on your breathing, she will go away."*

The ego loves it when we *resist* these glittery rewards, for our very resistance constitutes adequate distraction to avoid meditation.

> *I'm having strange images, like my whole body turning slowly upside down. Then I saw my whole aura, enveloping my body . . . I saw white swirls in the blackness; afterwards my legs were heavy . . . I had a dreamlike visualization of a silver Amtrak train full of people passing me quickly in bright sunshine.*

A useful device for disconnecting the ego in this mental tug-of-war is to become a consciousness watching this consciousness rather than *being* it. In other words, let your meditating self observe your busy, problem-solving mind.

This busy mind, with its parade of distractions, is often disturbing to new meditators. Beginners can be reassured that if the busy mind is so full of thoughts, problems, and anxieties, the mere attempt to meditate and process these distractions is a mind-clearing and cleansing process. After several days of meditation, the mind will be less alarmed by quiet periods, and it will allow more space between distracting thoughts. Even falling asleep during meditation is an important message to hear.

> *At first it feels like my body is having a temper tantrum, knowing it has to sit for a whole 15 minutes and concentrate on a single thing—being fully awake—it seems to get upset, like this is an insurmountable task. It makes me feel like I have a cranky 4-year-old inhabiting my body. I itch quite badly during the initial stages, and yawn quite a bit.*

Meditation needs space between thoughts. If it can get a little space, the meditation itself will widen and expand it. But there are times when distractions appear overwhelming in strength and frequency. You may have to meet the needs of these distractions before you can give meditation the foothold it needs. One way to do this is to stop the meditation and deal with the distracting thoughts. Or if you feel that you are falling asleep while meditating, stop and take a nap. Then, if at all possible, use the remaining space of time for a short meditation with your mind clear and/or rested.

Distractions are not the principal barrier to meditation; it is our *reaction* to them that holds us back or speeds us on. Since self-coercion is itself a distraction of the highest order, most meditative practices recommend a gentle permissiveness regarding distracting thoughts. It is recommended that distracting thoughts be recognized when they come. Recognize distractions as you would a passing acquaintance—but don't turn and follow them.

Thoughts should not be forced away. This is a primary emphasis in the Stream, Bubble, and 1,000 Petal Lotus meditations (pp. 62, 63, 67). In the early stages, you'll soon discover how many distracting thoughts can be entertained, and how controlling they are until gently mastered.

If, on a particular day, you feel bombarded with distractions coming from your personal life, stop your meditation, take a pad and pencil, and make a list of these distractions. Once you have listed your distractions, you can clear your mind of them, and still know that you will be able to remember them and deal with them later. This is a clearing process that some meditators use regularly.

> *I went to my safe harbor again today. I like it there. It was like a big daydream, and people could come in and out of the house, slamming doors and blasting music, and it didn't affect me. It was as though magic earplugs come with meditation, that just tune everything out.*

TIMING

We seem to have lots of time to meditate when we least need it, on vacations and during extended periods of relaxation. When we need meditation most, during busy stress periods, we are inclined to say that we don't have time. What we're really saying is "Meditation isn't a high enough *priority* for me—it can wait." Once meditation becomes important to us, we'll always have time for it.

Frequency

Healthy meditation is like healthy dieting. It thrives on constancy and must be faithfully adhered to or its benefits will not build. In the exercises of this book, most meditations should be done as a daily discipline for at least two weeks, and even that is merely an introduction to their benefits. There is no particular benefit to performing a meditation only once, unless you merely want to see what it's like. Don't miss a single day of meditation.

Time of Day

For best conditioned response to meditation and for ease in carrying out the discipline, one should (if possible) meditate at the same time or times each day. Once or twice a day is sufficient.

Some people like mid-morning and late afternoon for meditation. Late afternoon is a good time for washing away the accumulated tensions of the day and getting a "second wind" for the evening. Some use meditation instead of a customary afternoon nap, and claim to get more energy from the meditation than from the nap. Sunrise and sunset are good times for meditation. But late evening is usually not favored because meditation increases alertness and might make it difficult to fall asleep.

It is not recommended to meditate on a full stomach. After meals, our minds tend to be sluggish and our bodies are preoccupied. Many people who are attempting to lose weight meditate before or instead of eating. Meditation breaks the social expectation of eating, occupies the meal period, and provides both serenity and energy to the hungry dieter.

Duration

Fifteen- to twenty-minute periods of meditation are most effective. In the early stages, shorter meditations seem better than longer ones. One way to keep from falling asleep during meditation is to shorten the duration and increase the frequency. Similarly, if you experience significant discomfort during meditation (such as eyestrain), you may prefer shorter sessions.

Meditation teachers do warn against lengthy meditation that is unsupervised. When meditations last three to four hours, it is important to have a teacher involved.

> I have a private theory about length of meditation sessions. One of the qualities of meditation is that time seems to dissolve and disappear. My "when-you're-wet-you're-wet" theory is that once in the water, you're as wet as you're going to be. I believe that most concentrative meditation time is spent getting into the water; that is, reaching the level of immersion that yields results. Time inside the meditation is largely irrelevant. For this reason, I am a devotee of the five-minute mini-meditation, once you have learned to drop quickly into it.

Timing the Meditation

Fuss or anxiety about timing your own meditation can intrude on your concentration. A clock or watch nearby is all you need. Look at it occasionally until your time is up. An alarm is not necessary. After a few sessions, most people develop a natural sense of when to end a meditation.

Starting and Stopping

Starting a meditation is easy. Find your posture, relax, look around, and get settled. Think of your method, your purpose, and how you're breathing. Then take a few slow, deep breaths and sink into your concentration.

Stopping should be equally dignified. Meditation is not a trance, but it is a shift of consciousness sufficient to deserve some respect. When you finish a meditation, make sure you have allotted enough time to emerge from it slowly. You don't just snap it off like a light bulb. Return gradually to everyday thoughts. Rise leisurely. This applies also should you be interrupted while meditating. Allow yourself to surface slowly, as a deep-sea diver would. Don't jump up and rush off if you can avoid it.

POSTURE AND BREATHING

There are basically four postures mentioned in the many forms of meditation: chair sitting, cross-legged sitting, lying down, and standing/walking. (These postures exclude the active meditations such as Hatha Yoga, Tai Chi Chuan, Sufi, and the active Zen applications.)

The postures should allow free circulation of blood and energy and, like the consciousness that accompanies them, they should be alert and relaxed. It helps to wear loose, comfortable clothing and comfortable shoes. A common directive of many meditations is to keep the spine straight (in its natural curve) whether you are sitting, lying, or standing. Some followers of mystical disciplines believe that the spirit flows through the spine; others believe it flows in and out with the breathing.

Western, straight-chair sitting

Choose an upright but not restrictive chair. With your buttocks against the chair's back, sit straight, feet flat on the floor, and head tilted slightly down. Use the chair back as support if you need it.

Unless you're using your hands in meditation, let them rest on your thighs. A technique I enjoy is sitting with hands palms up, thumbs out. (Or you may rest your hands on your stomach. As your fingers feel your inner breathing, you're likely to feel a greater sense of wholeness.)

In any position you choose, feel free to scratch, move, shift, or stretch as needed.

Eastern cross-legged sitting

The cross-legged posture, known as the half- or full-lotus position, can be very comfortable if done correctly. In the half lotus, you sit cross-legged with one foot resting on the opposite thigh and crossing the other leg underneath. In the more difficult full lotus, your left foot rests on your right thigh, your right foot on your left thigh.

In either position, the secret to comfort is to sit on a stiff cushion (or folded fabric) that raises the buttocks about four inches off the floor; elevating the body reduces stress on the legs.

Meditators use various hand positions with the lotus. The prayer positions—thumbs pressed against index fingers, and clasped hand position—are believed to recirculate energy rather than letting it escape through the ends of the fingers.

Unless you're using one of these hand positions, it's okay to let your hands lie in your lap, one cupped palm up, the other resting palm down across that cup.

Lying, Standing, and Walking

Select postures which are comfortable and non-distracting. Obviously, lying on your back could put you to sleep. If you do lie down, keep the spine straight.

Any concentrative meditation can be done standing up. Though standing meditations are uncommon, they are thought to increase sensory awareness. Zen has a pleasant and controlled walking meditation. You'll be interested to know, too, that cloisters of Western monasteries and cathedrals were designed for walking meditation; in earlier times, meditators needed to *walk* to stay warm and active in cold weather!

I was recently delighted to see a sign in a large metropolitan airport that read "Meditation Room →." I followed the arrow to another sign and another, up and down stairs, around corners, along balconies, down long empty halls, through fire doors, etc. I was intent on finding this "Meditation Room." Then I realized I was right back where I had started from. I hadn't found the meditation room, but I had, in fact, done a very plausible walking meditation in search of it!

Breathing

Breathing is a discipline itself in some forms of meditation. As you meditate, you'll find that your breathing will become slower and take in less air. Breathing through the nose is advisable.

Attention to breathing is useful as a way of easing into meditation. Of course, in the Breath Counting meditation, you focus entirely on that process. While meditating, let your breathing become relaxed and natural, so that the movement is mainly in the abdomen, not the chest.

THE CONTENT-LESS THOUGHT

Over centuries, disciples of meditation have discovered a basic truth about the human mind which has been verified: no two thoughts can occupy the mind simultaneously. If you hold one single thought in your mind, it will serve to shut out all other thoughts. When you believe you're thinking more than one thought at a time, it's likely that you're experiencing the triphammer speed with which the mind can change from one thought to another, and back again. Taking that into consideration, concentrative meditation trains the mind to hold and unite with one thought, thus clearing the mind of all others.

But of course, holding even one thought is not truly clearing the mind. That's why most meditation forms embrace an important mental trick: *holding a thought that in itself has no content.* Even though you are holding a thought, the extent to which that thought has no content is the extent to which you are clearing your mind. It's much like keeping a telephone line open to prevent other calls. (Remember not to confuse concentrative meditation with advanced meditation, in which content is often significant.)

This meditative device has broad applications. "Busy" thoughts aren't required when you count numbers or concentrate on breathing. In single point meditation, you do not have to think about or "verbalize" the subject, but simply put your full attention on it. Similarly, the mantra is a repeatedly spoken syllable or phrase, often having no provocative meaning to the meditator. The content in each meditation must be attended to, but produces no chain of thoughts.

The same principle applies to individual and group prayer, chanting, or dancing. In prayers of Western religion (from the Lord's Prayer to rituals such as the Rosary), the prayer is repeated so often that it tends to lose content, but still requires one's attention. Whirling dervishes rotate to the monotonous chant of "Allah hu." And in both Hatha Yoga and Tai Chi Chuan, the meditator is so engrossed in remembering his or her sequence of movements that no substantive thought dares enter the mind.

REFERENCE

1. Claudio Naranjo and Robert Ornstein, *On the Psychology of Meditation* (New York: Viking Press, 1971).

Side Trip #4
SENSORY MEDITATIONS

The following six types of sensory meditations are effective as short, single point meditations. They also increase awareness of the unity of mind and body:

1. *Sound.* Search for a clear, simple sound that you can fully attend to, such as ringing in your ears, a simple musical instrument like a flute, wind chimes, a machine, or a purring engine. Meditate on this sound alone.

2. *Touch.* You may meditate on your own pulse, or the wind against your face. Try feeling an object with your eyes closed.

3. *Smell.* Meditate on the smell of incense, light perfume, the fragrance of a flower, or the pleasant aroma of food cooking. A natural scent is considered best.

4. *Taste.* When alone, you can meditate fully on the taste of what you are eating: chocolate, cheese, wine, an olive, etc. Taste the substance, then hold the taste as long as you can—as though it were the sound of a dying gong. Then take another taste and attend to it fully.

5. *Kinetic Meditation.* Sit with eyes open or closed. Allow your head to bob up or down slightly and keep time by tapping one foot. Keep all of your movements light. Use little energy. Focus on the movement and the rhythm. Continue for ten minutes.

6. *Kinesthetic Meditation.* Sit or lie down. Let your hands rest on your chest or abdomen, fingers spread but relaxed. Attend to the feeling of energy beneath your fingers. Continue it for ten minutes.

VI.

TEN WEEKS OF MEDITATION

How long it takes to "learn" meditation differs for everyone, but ten weeks will tell you what you want to know about your own acceptance or resistance to it, and whether meditation can make a positive change in your life large enough to be self-sustaining.

The five side trips in this book are good exercises to be used as often as you like. But the six main meditations included are proper forms and, though pleasant, they require discipline. The meditations are listed in order of increasing variety and difficulty. I recommend that you not skip any or change the order.

SPECIALTIES OF EACH MEDITATION

All concentrative meditation exercises are designed to clear, expand, and unify mind and body. Yet each meditation has its own unique purpose. Once you have worked with them all, you'll begin to know which meditations best suit your current needs.

1. The Breath Counting Meditation–
A fundamental meditation to practice focusing on one thought. (Weeks One and Two)

2. The Stream Meditation–
Helps clear the mind when one is particularly tense and pre-occupied. It dissolves distractions. (Weeks Three and Four)

3. The Single Point Meditation–
Aims at providing a sense of internal and external unity and full awakeness. (Weeks Five and Six)

4. The 1,000 Petal Lotus Meditation–
A processing exercise to discover what thoughts are clustering around a single large concept of one's life. (Weeks Seven and Eight)

5. The Mantra Meditation–
Emphasizes the inner unity of the body, mind, and senses. The resonance of the mantra reinforces this union. (Week Nine)

6. The Zen of Doing–
Applies meditation to one's daily activities. It unifies *being* and *doing.* (Week Ten)

A Simple Retreat

When the assigned daily meditation seems beyond your ability to concentrate (whether it's because you're tense, preoccupied, tired, or not feeling well), you can turn to the Safe Harbor meditation. It is effortless, reassuring, and calming. Some use it as a substitute after a hard day, some use it as a preparation for their regular meditation.

First Meditation: Weeks One and Two
THE BREATH COUNTING MEDITATION

This meditation is described in full on pages 2-3.

Do not let the apparent ease and simplicity of the breath counting meditation cause you to underestimate it. It is not child's play but a fully functional meditation form. Some meditators use it exclusively and never need another form.

Changing Meditations

Meditators tend to become attached and loyal to the meditations they have learned to perform. Yet, different meditation styles have different processes and different effects as well. Make this clear to yourself whenever you stop one meditation style and start another by saying this to yourself: "I am about to try a different meditation. It will be like starting again. I am ready for a new experience."

After the first two weeks of the breath counting meditation, continue with the following meditations.

Second Meditation: Weeks Three and Four
THE STREAM MEDITATION

---

1. Find your meditation place.

2. Sit comfortably straight in a chair or cross-legged on the floor, or lie down.

3. Place your timepiece.

4. Slow down, relax, and take six long, slow breaths.

5. Close your eyes.

6. Start your meditation: Picture yourself sitting by a stream as it slowly passes you. The stream is in a peaceful glade, with trees overhead, long, limp grass on the banks, smooth rocks along the stream edge, and sunny warmth from above. There are leaves floating past on the current of the stream. They appear from upstream, float gently by, and disappear downstream.

    Focus entirely on the stream and the leaves. If any other thought comes to your mind, place the thought (or a single word representing that thought) on a leaf and let it float through your mind, disappearing with the leaf. No leaf stays before you, and no thought stays in your mind. If there is no distracting thought, merely let the leaves pass through.

    If a thought returns, put it on a second leaf and float it through your mind again. Do this until it stops returning. Over time, there will be fewer and fewer leaves on the stream, as less thoughts occupy your mind. Eventually, the stream—and your mind—will be entirely clear of leaves (thoughts).

7. Stay awake. Hold your posture.

8. Meditate for 15 minutes.

9. Stop meditating. Return to your normal thoughts and activities gradually.

10. What happened? How do you feel?

The purpose of this meditation is to help you pass thoughts and feelings through without rejecting them, but without hanging on to them or letting them connect to new thoughts.

There are variations of the stream meditation, and one of them may feel more natural for you:

- Picture yourself on the bank of a broad river as logs float downstream. The logs are thoughts. Let them pass and disappear. (Tibetan)

- Picture yourself sitting on the bottom of a pool, or clear lake, and having no trouble breathing there. Large bubbles are coming into view at the bottom and rising silently and slowly to the surface, taking five or more seconds to reach the top. Each bubble holds a thought, feeling, or perception of yours. Observe each one rise and wait for the next one. Don't search for thoughts to place in the bubbles; some bubbles will rise empty. If a thought returns, place it in another bubble and let it rise again out of your consciousness. Let the bubbles rise slowly, regularly, and rhythmically.

Undated log: I had a horrible day today. In an effort to calm my anger I tried to meditate. Fifteen minutes later all my negative energy was released. Like blind mice, I led every negative thought out of my mind, one after the other.

Third Meditation: Weeks Five and Six
THE SINGLE POINT MEDITATION

---

1. Find a small, pleasing object to look at, natural or man-made: a flower, plant, rock, seashell, simple carving, vase, piece of hardware—nothing too ornate—something you can pick up and hold in your hands.

2. Find your meditation place.

3. Sit comfortably straight.

4. Place your object directly in front of you or hold it in your hand. (This is your first eyes-open meditation.)

5. Place your timepiece.

6. Slow down, relax, and take six long, slow breaths.

7. Start your meditation: Look at your object without staring and without commenting on it to yourself. Just look at the object as though you're initiating a bond with it.

8. In rhythm with your slow breathing, say silently to yourself the words "This" (as you inhale) and "Now" (as you exhale). The unvoiced mantra is to direct you constantly to your object. (During the second week, you may stop saying "This" and "Now" to yourself, if you wish.)

9. Recognize distractions and come back to your object without guilt, to look, breathe, and think "THIS. NOW."

10. Stay awake. Hold your posture.

11. Meditate for fifteen minutes.

12. Stop meditating. Return to your normal thoughts and activities slowly.

13.   What happened? How do you feel?

14.   Resume the meditation tomorrow—same time, same duration, same object, and same place, if possible.

How to Look at the Object

One of the Chinese words for meditation means "union of me and the object." This applies here. Let your eyes rest on the object. Try to see it as it exists in itself, without any connection to other things. Let perception alone fill your mind. Look innocently, as a child would. You may look away occasionally so that you aren't tempted to stare at it. Look, but don't stare. Move or turn the object if you like. Try not to let your seeing drop back into your head.

The meditation object is not supposed to take you on a nostalgic trip, as in remembering the day you found the seashell on the beach. It is what it is, not what it was, where it has been, or what has been associated with it. Single point is *nonassociative*.

Place the object in front of a plain background to minimize distraction. Do not use a flame or light as your object. In fact, it is best to face away from any direct sources of light. Subdued lighting is best.

Choosing Your Object

Once you have found a pleasing object, continue to use it. If you will meditate on the same object each day, in the same place at the same time, you will start to develop a conditioned response and each day move more quickly into the meditation. Once you have chosen an object for single point meditation, try to keep it out of sight for the rest of the day so that you only see it when meditating.

Any object that is pleasant and does not have too much detail or association connected with it will do. Trainers in this style have used everything from match sticks to doorknobs and personal jewelry; a standard object is a small blue vase.

Some of the appropriate objects selected by new meditators are: a pine cone, a crystal, an orange, an egg, a smooth rock, a feather, a seashell, and a rose. Objects such as a trophy, a watch, a piggy bank, a pencil eraser, a marble (too small), a photograph, a toy car, and a piece of the Berlin Wall arouse too many associations and memories to be effective as objects of meditation.

Single point meditation is one of the most widely used of all meditations. It is strongly keyed to the here and now.

Although new meditators are occasionally put off for a day or two by meditating with their eyes open, they soon report being happily surprised by the increased focus of the visual meditation.

> **Undated log:** *As I stared at my plant, breathing deeply in and out, I could feel my tension leaving my body. I never realized before that just by doing this for 10 to 15 minutes a day I could feel this good about myself.*

> **Undated log:** *Today I feel as though I have a real connection with my seashell, as though it was connected to my hands. As I rotate it, I feel my breathing becoming more and more fluid. As I breathe, I can almost feel my breath penetrating the shell. I feel great as usual. I always feel so good after the meditation. I feel as though I am one with the shell.*

> **Day 7, with a sand dollar:** *Totally bizarre—I felt like I was actually the sand dollar—almost like the first time I felt really good from prayer.*

Fourth Meditation: Weeks Seven and Eight
THE 1,000 PETAL LOTUS MEDITATION

1. Find your meditation place.

2. Sit comfortably straight in a chair, cross-legged on the floor, or lie down.

3. Choose a single, central concept that is important to you, applies to you, or interests you, and that is without negative connections for you. Meditators regularly choose such concepts as love, family, success, road, tree, home, mountain, energy, work, leisure, choice, quality, freedom, time, or commitment.

   Do not use as central concepts specifics such as friends, lovers, or tasks. Choose the deeper, positive abstractions in you, like love, friendship, harmony, well-being, happiness, nature, etc.

4. Place your timepiece.

5. Slow down, relax, and take six long, slow breaths.

6. Close your eyes.

7. Start your meditation: Picture a lotus blossom, with a center and many petals surrounding it. Place your own central concept in the center of the lotus, contemplate it, and wait. When a thought associates with the concept, take the thought out onto the first petal of the lotus, stay with the thought for three or four seconds and then leave it, returning to the center of the lotus and your central concept.

   When the next thought occurs, take it out onto the second petal, observe it, and return. Continue on in this way.

You may or may not see the association between your central concept and each thought. It doesn't matter. What's important is to leave each thought and return to the central concept to wait for the next thought.

Do not use the lotus as a problem-solving device, a projection test of your categories, a vacation planner, or a morale booster. Meditation is a method of discharging thoughts, not calling them up for analysis.

8. Stay awake. Hold your posture.

9. Meditate for 15 minutes.

10. Stop meditating. Return to your normal thoughts and activities slowly.

11. What happened? How do you feel?

12. Use the same or a different central concept each time you meditate.

Unlike previous meditations, the 1,000 Petal Lotus meditation brings us closer to personal issues and interests. It often leads to surprising insights.

Your choice of a central concept is a key to effective results. Keep the concept general, not specific: positive or neutral, not negative. Search for unifying concepts, such as health, family, friendship, confidence, beauty, joy, or change. Negative concepts like anger, conflict, and sadness tend to produce a negative meditation.

The more abstract your central concept, the better. Let the petals be the places where specifics appear. The meditation is not intended to be a problem-solving session. Before starting, think to yourself, "Here is my broad, deep idea. Now let me see what's there ready to be looked at."

Do not search for the specifics or allow yourself to be put off by petal thoughts that appear to have nothing whatsoever to do with your central concept. Let the specific thoughts appear naturally, without criticism or censorship.

Fifth Meditation: Week Nine
THE MANTRA MEDITATION

1. Find your meditation place. Since you'll be voicing a sound, you'll need total privacy.

2. Sit comfortably straight in a chair or cross-legged.

3. Place your timepiece.

4. Slow down, relax, and take six long, slow breaths.

5. Close your eyes.

6. Start your meditation: As you exhale each breath, repeat one word aloud, but very softly. Draw it out for the entire exhalation. The word is "AUM." In it, you'll find the sounds "ah," "oh," and "mm." As you relax, your breaths will lengthen and so will the mantra. You'll then find it easier to change pitch until you've found the most natural, easy sound—the one that vibrates through your body. Focus on the chanting and nothing else, involving yourself more and more in the sound. Don't let it become automatic. Gradually, reduce the sound to a whisper, until it's not spoken at all, but only imagined. The sound does not have to be vocalized to make an impact.

7. Stay awake, hold your posture, and meditate for fifteen minutes.

8. Stop meditating. Return to your normal thoughts and activities slowly.

9. What happened? How do you feel?

In Sanskrit, "Mantra" means "thought form." It's believed that the power of the Deity lies in its name. In that search, 700,000 Sanskrit mantras have been recorded. Mantras are often used for such special purposes as illness, business, wealth, blessings, mathematics, mind-reading, love, courtship, and marriage. A mantra may have one or more syllables, phrases, or verses.

In its pure sense, mantra is said to be the "primordial sound of the Ultimate Reality." By repeating the sound "AUM" properly, one is creating the universe. "AUM" is considered to be the universal sound from which all other mantras spring.

In concentrative meditation, we're interested more in the effects of the actual sound produced than we are in the rewards of the mantra's content. (In advanced meditation, the content of the mantra is crucial.) The mantra is used as a "content-less thought." When properly intoned, the sound itself appears to resonate in both mind and body, where it creates an inner sense of unity and dramatic awareness. Chanting a mantra aloud with other meditators extends that unity, even when your partners use different rhythms and pitches. The secret of the mantra is said to lie in how it is chanted. Therefore, experimentation is useful.

A popular Western mantra is "ONE." Another is "ALL IS ONE." Recommended Eastern mantras are "RA-MA," "AH-NAM," or "SHI-RIM." When unvoiced, two-syllable mantras are usually divided so that the first syllable comes as you inhale, the second syllable as you exhale.

I was once sitting alone on the bow of a boat, winding up a narrow river, listening to the hum of the motor, a large outboard. I began to hum with the engine, experimenting with different pitches. Suddenly, my humming blended so perfectly with the motor sound that there was only one sound. In those few moments until I lost it, I was one with myself, the engine, the boat, the river, the trees, and all beyond. There was nothing that was not part of that unity, and the feeling was one of extraordinary harmony and peace.

My own students report struggling with the self-consciousness of the mantra sound for the first two days; then, on day three or four, they open up to it.

Day 1: *I felt really silly about making noise. I guess it is that it is noise without words. Anyway, I was glad there was nobody around to hear me. I kept changing my pitch, trying to find a comfortable one, but they all felt stiff and forced. I could never shake the self-observer.*

Day 2: *I felt more comfortable today. I relaxed into the sound my body was making and it felt more natural. I felt my whole throat and chest open up. I wasn't fighting myself. My voice resonated into clear elongated ringing. My voice still felt separate from me. It was more like I was listening to someone else.*

Day 3: *Much better today! I took my six breaths and from there I just let go into it. I dropped into a low timbre that I would not expect from myself, but that felt super comfortable and at-home. My voice vibrated through my chest and out into the world. I felt like I had found the cosmic resonating level and just became part of it.*

Day 4: *I really felt vulnerable today, like my defenses were gone and my soul was open to the world. I did not feel threatened though, just raw—wide open. Then it felt like the universe wrapped its arms around me and I was whole because we were one. What an incredible feeling.*

Day 7: *I once again had a terrific experience. My flesh and soul just melted away and blurred with the universe. I felt like sky itself, endless, boundless space. My voice felt like universal harmony, the lynch pin shared by all, what connected me to everything else.*

Day 3: *As I went into my meditation, I heard the sounds of my breaths and it felt as if it was mystical. My chanting followed . . . It is very difficult to explain. It was as though* a big hand had picked me up gently and carried me over to a calm tranquil area. After my fifteen minutes, I felt totally peaceful with my surroundings.

Day 3: Today, while meditating, I lost the feeling in me as my voice came out. I felt nothing but my sounds. It was fantastic. It was like I wasn't really there. Only a sound. When I came back (which took a while to come into my body again) I was so relaxed. It was as though my body had taken a rest, because I was ready to work again.

Day 3: As I meditated I seemed to be connected to the ground. I felt very secure. The mantra (my exhale) became longer and more quiet as I meditated. The mantra just seems to stop when it becomes inaudible. Instead of forcing myself to go on I just follow what seems right. I just sit in a very calm, relaxed state for the next five minutes. The environment seems good, even the traffic noise. The meditation makes me very aware of the here and now.

Day 5: This mantra makes me feel the most naked of all the meditations. It is the only one that is both internal and external.

Day 8: I'm not embarrassed to do this meditation anymore. I feel this meditation is a portrait of me. If I'm embarrassed about performing the meditation, then I'm embarrassed about me.

Undated: Wow! I finally felt "oneness" tonight during meditation. While I was verbalizing "Aum" I was really feeling it, not just saying it. I was thinking "Aum" and I was feeling "Aum." So now I think I am truly starting to understand the idea of the mind and body becoming one.

Sixth Meditation: Week Ten
THE ZEN OF DOING

You have had nine weeks of discipline in concentration, unifying thought with object of thought, holding to a point, awake, alert and relaxed, gradually eliminating distraction. You have stopped everything else to meditate.

Now it's time to *apply* meditation directly to everything in your life, and to create a clear unity of self with action.

1. Choose a task that you know how to do and do often, but find difficult to do well. Examples include: cooking a recipe, writing a poem, cleaning house, driving a golf ball, playing tennis, and studying.

2. Select a period of time in which to do the task—a period of time that is at least twice as long as you would think normal for the task. This is to ensure that time will not be a distraction for you. The meditation should be open-ended in time.

3. Prepare perfectly for the task. Anticipate all the tools and materials you'll need and have them in perfect condition, arranged for use. (Make your work space clean, well-lit, and free of distraction.)

4. Set up a meditation area directly in front of (or in the midst of) the job to be done, along with all its tools and materials.

5. Start your meditation: use the directions for a single point meditation with the silent mantra "ONE." In this case, the object of the meditation is unity with the task at hand.

6. Allow a minimum of five or ten minutes for the meditation. When you feel alert, undistractedly in the here and now, and *at one with the task,* get up and do it.

7. Each day, repeat the task, if appropriate, or choose a different task.

Zen Buddhism is famous for its application to the arts and to special skills like brush-painting, haiku poetry, flower arranging, the tea ceremony, and the arts of archery and swordsmanship. But Zen is also known as an intensely practical and active discipline. In Zen, the mind is trained in hours of tranquil meditation and then applied to life around it.

Zen method is not merely for the arts; it is the application of Zen that can raise any worthwhile task to an art. This means that whatever you do, there is available to you "The Zen of..." (doing it): cooking, walking, selling, tennis, carpentry, motorcycle maintenance, computer programming, surfboarding, teaching, writing, composing and playing an instrument. Zen in the arts includes the concept that anything worth doing as a part of your life is also worthy of being an art, a complete absorption of the moment, and is adaptable to the principles of Zen discipline.

The Zen of "Anything" involves four tasks:

1. *Preparation*
   a. The perfect adjustment of environment and layout of tools
   b. Open-ended time: don't use this if you're "running late"
   c. Physical readiness: be as ready as you would be for a journey

2. *Concentration*
   a. Meditation upon the task: use single point meditation, allowing yourself to be fully absorbed by the task
   b. Saturation with the task: push out distraction (by having full absorption of the task). (The Zen painter "goes to the mountain" in his mind before he paints it)

3. *Integration*
   a. Merge the goal, the process, and the ego into one
   b. You (ego) are not directing the process, but joining it
   c. When all is one, you are ready

4. *Execution*
   a. Stay in the here and now
   b. Go with the flow—adapt, be flexible; everything that happens is equally necessary

My students amaze me with the diversity of tasks to which they effectively apply the Zen of Doing. Some of their recent projects are listed on the next page:

writing	yoga
correspondence	salad making
vacuuming	surfing
Christmas shopping	telephone solicitation
jogging	cleaning the bathroom
brushing the cat	reading textbooks
novel reading	playing guitar
shaving legs	script writing
homework	knitting
doing dishes	washing hair
long-distance driving	car washing
ironing	dieting
shooting baskets	body-building exercises
skipping rope	performance dancing
driving to work	making the bed
making chocolate-chip cookies	paying monthly bills
going to court	television/film-editing

In Zen, the perfection you seek in anything is in itself a unity, and you a unity of that unity. You and the task and all its parts are one. When you understand this, you also understand the Zen direction to the archer pulling his bow that the arrow and the target are one; it is the task of the archer to release the arrow in such a way as not to interfere with that unity.

You cannot find this unity of being and doing without being fully awake and totally into the moment, the here and now. No other thoughts but the unity of artist, process, and time must be allowed. Not only do you eliminate all external distractions, but you also eliminate the distraction of any separateness within the unity: you fuse into one the artist (yourself) and the task (the process) in its moment of time (the here and now). The result is a doing that does itself, intentionless and natural, without the busy "do- er" of the ego.

In the Zen of Doing, time is suspended. A Zen process can only be done in the here and now. Time itself exists only by virtue of its being divided into past, present, and future. Thoughts of past and future distract us from the here and now. If you're a potter at the wheel, there's only you, the clay, the tools, and the process in the here and now. Even the final product—a beautiful pot— exists in the here and now, in the potter's mind.

> ***The Zen of Writing:*** *I put my clipboard with paper on it and a pen on top of the paper in front of me and meditated on writing, saying "one." I couldn't believe it, but it worked. Before the meditation, I had, sort of, a writing block (more of procrastination, I think). Anyway, I did the meditation and began writing and the words and thoughts really flowed. I wrote for a couple of hours nonstop. I feel the meditation really unblocked my creativity. I took a dinner break and came back, finished the paper, and wrote another one late into the evening. What amazed me is I didn't get tired; I was full of energy and very alert.*

> ***Undated log:*** *This was definitely different. I tried it right before studying. I set all of my things out on the kitchen table—books, paper, pen, typewriter, etc. I tried concentrating with my pen in my hand. I had one major paper to write. I concentrated on the word "one." After about ten minutes, I stopped and began writing. Maybe it's my imagination, but I could have sworn that my mind was more unblocked and it was easier to write.*

> *O.K. What a difference this stuff makes. I did the Zen meditation right before I began vacuuming. Amazingly for me, I did not stop cleaning for 2 hours straight (except to answer the phone). I actually got everything accomplished.*

> *I feel so in tune with my studies today. This meditation is like organizing my entire plan of action before going through with it. I feel that this is what I've needed all along.*

I had a student who, although good-natured, had no interest in meditation. He did, however, have a rabid interest in making surfboards in his garage. He had a problem in that at a certain point in the building of a surfboard he had to make a series of precise cuts. If he made them wrong, the whole board and days of previous work were ruined. His anxiety about this became so intense that when he approached the crucial cutting task, he froze. He could no longer perform. He adopted the Zen of Doing in the following way:

1. He prepared the task so that when he began the process, he wouldn't be distracted. He cleared his work space and cleaned trash underfoot. Like a surgeon, he repaired, sharpened, and laid out every tool he would need. He arranged perfect lighting and set up the work piece so that it was firmly fixed in its most workable position.

2. He selected a work time that was free from interruptions, obligations, or appointments. He agreed to release thoughts of time.

3. He slowed down. During the work period, he allowed the process to lead him. He did not push or hurry it.

4. Finally, he meditated on the unity of the process. He set up a meditation place in full view of his workplace and tools.

5. Once he felt a sense of unity with himself, his tools, and his task, he began his work.

6. Whenever he felt he had lost his here-and-now unity, he was to stop working, leave the project, and begin again at a later time.

Preparation
    Time
        Relaxation
            Meditation
                Unity
                    Here and Now

The process worked for him. He dissolved his anxiety, performed the crucial cutting necessary, and raised the task to an art.

Side Trip #5
TAI CHI CHUAN

Tai Chi Chuan is a meditation I cannot teach you in print; you will have to go to a teacher. Nevertheless, I include it here because it represents to me an apex in concentrative meditation in its focused multi-dimensionality. It unites body, mind, and spirit. Tai Chi is an active, precise, totally involving, slow-motion dance.

Tai Chi Chuan has very unmeditative beginnings, for the dance of Tai Chi is said to have evolved from an ancient martial art, developed by the Chinese aristocracy to defend themselves against bandits while traveling the roads. Tai Chi is slow-motion shadowboxing, for every movement is in anticipation of one or more imaginary opponents. It was one of the soft rather than hard martial arts, in that its purpose was to allow your opponent to do anything he wished to do without its hurting you, based on three martial arts principles: to adhere, to yield, and to discharge.

Eventually, the Chinese aristocracy did not need to train themselves in personal defense, but rather than give up the art completely, they continued to teach it to themselves as a meditative dance, in strenuously slow motion. There are now multiple styles and short and long forms (from ten to thirty minutes in length), and the forms are so precise that it is often done in perfect unison by groups of people. In addition to its personal benefits, it is aesthetically beautiful. Tai Chi Chuan is so currently popular as a form of physical fitness and meditation among the older generation in Asia that it has been called "the old man's dance."

One does Tai Chi Chuan daily, preferably early in the morning— indoors or out. Its value to concentrative meditation is this: to follow the ritual, using the entire body simultaneously, directed by a mind that cannot for a moment lose its place in the sequence, is to effectively shut out all distraction.

Everyday life effects of Tai Chi are interesting. The body becomes more graceful, strong, and flowing— the mind, calm, and more secure. An investment in time (about three months) and money is necessary to learn Tai Chi from a master, but I believe it to be a supreme form of concentrative meditation.

VII.

CONCLUSION

Your experience is the conclusion of this book. If you have followed the recommended course for ten weeks, you have something to say about what has changed in you, in your perceptions, and in your life and work.

If you have merely read this book, you'll have nothing to say but lots to talk about. People have to be *ready* for meditation, I think, as they have to be ready for marriage. Both take some maturity, curiosity, a desire for more, strong intention, and hope. And both have to be experienced before one knows anything important about them.

If you have tried all six of the major meditations, you may now be able to decide which were your best and which your worst. You may wish to divide the meditations into:

1.   those you will do regularly

2.   those you will do on occasion, as needed

3.   those you are not likely to repeat, but remain open to

4.   those you feel are not right for you

If you like the six meditations all equally, then you will understand this student comment, that seems to say it all:

"After every meditation, it is like opening my eyes to a new world."

RECOMMENDED READING

Patricia Carrington, *Freedom in Meditation* (Garden City, N.Y.: Doubleday, Anchor Press, 1977).

Arthur J. Deikman, "Experimental Meditation": in Charles Tart, ed., *Altered States of Consciousness* (New York: John Wiley & Sons, 1969), pp. 199-218.

Eugene Herrigel, *Zen in the Art of Archery* (New York: Pantheon Books, 1953).

Lawrence LeShan, *How to Meditate* (New York: Bantam Books paperback, 1974).

Edward W. Maupin, "On Meditation," in Charles Tart, ed., *Altered States of Consciousness* (New York: John Wiley & Sons, 1969), pp. 177-186.

Claudio Naranjo and Robert Ornstein, *On the Psychology of Meditation* (New York: Viking Press, 1971).

Jacob Needleman, *The New Religions* (New York: Crossroads Publishing Co., 1984).

Alan Watts, *The Way of Zen* (New York: Mentor Books, 1957).

John White, ed., *What is Meditation?* (New York: Anchor Books, 1974).

Ken Wilbur, *Eye To Eye, The Quest for the New Paradigm* (New York: Doubleday, Anchor Press, 1983).

OTHER BOOKS BY ARTHUR HOUGH

The Forgotten Choice: Breaking Through Paradigm to Human Potential (San Francisco, 1988). Self-published and copyrighted.

Let's Have It Out: The Bare-Bones Manual of Fair Fighting (Minneapolis, Minn.: CompCare Publishers, 1991).

Pulling Yourself Together": A Brief Guide to Resolving Inner Conflicts through Subself Negotiation (Minneapolis, Minn: CompCare Publishers, 1991).